TRUE CRIME

# BREAKOUTS AND BLUNDERS

John Townsend

# www.raintreepublishers.co.uk

Visit our website to find out more information about **Raintree** books.

To order:

☎ Phone 44 (0) 1865 888113

▤ Send a fax to 44 (0) 1865 314091

▣ Visit the Raintree Bookshop at **www.raintreepublishers.co.uk** to browse our catalogue and order online.

First published in Great Britain by
Raintree, Halley Court, Jordan Hill, Oxford OX2 8EJ,
part of Harcourt Education.
Raintree is a registered trademark of Harcourt
Education Ltd.

Editorial: Melanie Copland and Sarah Chappelow
Design: Lucy Owen and Kamae Design
Picture Research: Hannah Taylor and Ginny Stroud-
Lewis
Production: Duncan Gilbert

Originated by RMW
Printed and bound in China
by South China Printing Company

ISBN 1 844 43812 0
11 10 09 08 07 06
10 9 8 7 6 5 4 3 2 1

**British Library Cataloguing in Publication Data**
Townsend, John
Breakouts and Blunders – (True Crime)
365.6'41
A full catalogue record for this book is available from
the British Library.

**Acknowledgements**
Alamy Images pp. **10** (Dennis Hallinan), **10–11** (Pixoi),
**13** (Mikael Karlsson), **14** (Jack Sullivan), **17** (Stephen
Saks Photography), **23** (Todd Bannor), **30–31** (Ingram
Publishing), **32–33** (Shout), **35** (Brand X Pictures/Steve
Allen), **38–39** (Shout), **39** (D Hurst), **40** (Andy Myatt),
**41** (Mikael Karlsson), **42** (Billy Hall), **44–45** (Ingram
Publishing), **5** (Brand X Pictures), **5** top (Shout), **8-9**
(Image Source); Associated Press pp. **15** (Oded Balilty),
**28**, **29** top, **29** bottom, **33**; Corbis pp. **title**, **4** (Dave
Teel), **5** (Terry W. Eggers), **6–7** (Paul Colangelo), **7**,
**11**, **12**, **12–13** (Kim Kulish), **14–15** (Reuters), **19**, **20**
(Douglas Peebles), **20-21** (Terry W. Eggers), **24**
(Bettmann), **26** (Hulton-Deutsch Collection), **27**
(Reuters), **31** (Tim Wright), **34**, **36** (Mitchell Gerber);
Getty Images pp. **5** bottom (Photodisc), **6** (Stone),
**42–43** (Photodisc); Harcourt Education Ltd pp. **8**
(Tudor Photography), **9** (Ginny Stroud-Lewis); Mary
Evans Picture Library pp. **18**, **19**; Science Photo
Library p. **37** (Scott Camazine); The Kobal Collection
pp. **16** (Castle Rock Entertainment), **22**
(Paramount/Malpaso), **22–23**, **25** (Castle Rock/Warner
Bros/Nelson, Ralph Jr), **26–27** (Embassy), **34–35**
(Polygram/Spelling), **43**.

Cover photograph of a prison cell reproduced with
permission of Corbis/Terry W. Eggers.

# Contents

Any words appearing in the text in bold, **like this**, are explained in the Glossary. You can also look out for them in the Word Bank at the bottom of each page.

# Oops!

## Failed

Prisons are full of criminals. The reason they are behind bars is because their crimes failed or were found out. Some prisoners go on to make matters worse. They try to escape from prison. Very few prisoners succeed in escaping – they usually fail again!

There is a saying that "crime does not pay". It is certainly not a very wise **career** choice! Not many criminals end up living happily ever after. Even if they never get caught, they can spend their lives hiding, waiting to be found out. They fear the next knock on the door. Life on the run can be tough.

It only takes one mistake for even the cleverest criminal to end up in prison. But it seems some criminals make more mistakes than others!

## Unwise

Many criminals want to get rich quick, without getting caught. But there is no such thing as a perfect crime. Something usually ends up going wrong.

Sometimes criminals make silly mistakes and get caught. Once in prison, some criminals try to escape. Not a good idea! Things nearly always go horribly wrong. **Breakouts** often turn into **blunders**!

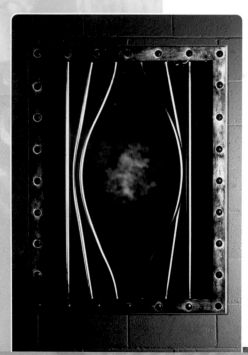

**Word Bank**

blunder  silly mistake, when things go wrong
breakout  escape

Crime does not pay!

## Find out later...

How many criminals go through the roof?

Which prison was almost impossible to escape from?

How did a gorilla catch a thief?

# Big mistakes

Bungling burglars appear in many comedy films. They also appear in real life.

## Just plain crazy

There is a story about a very nervous bank robber called Paul Bernier. The 32-year-old used a toy gun to rob a bank in Swansea, Massachusetts, USA. When the bank cashier told him she had no money, he fainted. He was out cold when the police arrived to arrest him.

## Gang in robbery blunder (September 2004)

A gang of robbers was arrested in Salvador, Brazil after trying to rob a shop. As they ran in, one of the robbers dropped a gun, which went off. It shot him in the leg and scared the other robbers, who ran off. They tried to escape on motorbikes, but crashed into each other and fell off. One of the police officers that arrested the robbers said: "They were the funniest and easiest criminals to catch. They were so goofy and messy, we were all laughing".

Making a quick getaway went horribly wrong in Brazil

**Word Bank**  disguise change the way you look to hide from, or fool, other people

# Bank robber asks for a lift

In 2004, Ernest Di Falco tried to rob a bank in Rutherford, New Jersey, USA. The 53-year-old wore sunglasses and a long brown wig. After he had robbed the bank, he asked one of the cashiers for a lift to his getaway car. Instead, the cashier ordered him a taxi. When it arrived, bank staff took its number and told the police.

Despite Di Falco's **disguise**, a cashier had recognized him as a worker in a nearby pizza shop. Police soon arrested him. He still had the bank's money, a gun, and bullets. He was charged with armed robbery. In the United States, the punishment for this is up to 20 years in prison.

## Unlucky

Frank Gort, a burglar from San Antonio, Texas, USA, was found **guilty** of robbery in court. The judge gave him a 7-year prison sentence. Gort was very upset, and begged the judge to change his mind, as seven was his unlucky number. The judge kindly agreed. He gave him 8 years instead!

Judges send criminals to prison every day.

**guilty** done something wrong

In December 2002,
a burglar called
Mark Cossington
broke into a house
in Suffolk, UK. He
made a silly mistake
while he was there.
He left behind his
own front door key.
It had a label with
his name on it.
Police soon gave
him a call. He was
jailed for three and
a half years.

## Hitting the roof

In 2002, a burglar stole £100,000 of jewellery
from Harvey Nichols, a large department store
in London, UK. He broke in and gathered up the
jewels, but set off the alarm. He climbed through
a ceiling tile and hid. Police searched the store
with dogs while he lay still. He stayed still for
over 12 hours, hoping to escape the next night.
But during the afternoon a customer saw a
ceiling tile move. The police were called back
and the man was arrested. His next night was
more comfortable. It was in a proper bed …
in a police cell.

Leaving behind
clues like this is a
big **blunder**!

Harvey Nichols in
London, where a
burglar made a
big mistake.

## Sticking around

In February 2004 Mr Attala Abboushi opened his shop in Cleveland, Ohio, USA, and saw legs dangling from the ceiling. A burglar had tried to break in through the air vent and was firmly stuck. He had not been able to move for over 4 hours and was shouting for help. Mr Abboushi called police and firefighters who cut the burglar free. He was taken to hospital and then to the city police cells. Police thought the burglar had also broken into other shops in the area through their air vents – before he got stuck! He was charged with breaking and entering.

## Doh!

In Modesto, California, USA, Steven King was arrested for trying to rob a bank. King had no weapon, so he used a thumb and a finger in his pocket to look like he had a gun. The trouble was, he took out his hand to point it at the cashier. Doh!

A finger and thumb...not likely to fool anyone!

## Caught with his pants down

In February 2004, Aaron Reynolds was driving a stolen car into New York City, USA. When police stopped him, he ran off. Only two streets away, the police caught him when he fell over. His jeans had fallen down and tripped him up!

Reynolds told them he was giving up and asked to pull up his jeans. As he was doing so, he darted off again. He only got a few metres away when his jeans slipped down yet again, and down he fell. The police finally arrested him.

### Come and get me

In the United States, Marvin Stewart, a 76-year-old ex-convict really missed prison. He walked into a bank in Council Bluffs, Iowa and handed over a note demanding two US$50 bills. He left the bank and told staff he would be waiting outside in his car for police to come and take him back to prison.

One criminal was so desperate to escape he hid in a crate!

When someone has been in prison a very long time, they sometimes do not want to leave.

**Word Bank**    bribe  something given to a person, usually money, to make them do something dishonest

## The great escape?

Jonathan Schempp of Quincy, Massachusetts, had to go to court on 12 May 2004 for some motor **offences**. He decided to run away instead. So, he packed himself in a crate to be sent by ship to Cape Verde, Africa. He got a friend to deliver him in his crate to the shipping company's warehouse. But the plan went wrong. The shipping company nailed his crate shut and stacked other crates on top. He was soon running out of air and no one could hear his cries. The ship was delayed and, after 3 days, his worried friend called the police. Schempp was taken to hospital and arrested for missing his court date.

## Drive-in prison

In 1999, thieves in Florida, USA, took a wrong turn and ended up on the Homestead Air Force Base. They drove up to a military police guardhouse. They thought it was a ticket booth for paying to be let through. They gave the security men some of the stolen money ... and were arrested for trying to **bribe** an officer!

**offence** crime, something that breaks the law

# How to be a prisoner

For most criminals the biggest **blunder** is thinking about committing a crime in the first place. After all, they are likely to get caught, sooner or later.

## Under arrest

The police can arrest anyone who is creating a **disturbance**. If they have strong reasons to think someone has committed a crime, or is going to commit one, the police can make an arrest. If they give a warning and a **suspect** begins shouting back, an arrest is more likely. Already having a criminal record may make it more likely for someone to be arrested at the scene of a crime.

**Word Bank**

charge formal blame for a crime
disturbance something that upsets people or causes harm

# What happens next?

After being arrested, a suspect will be taken to a police station. The police will then decide whether to **charge** the suspect with a crime. Once at the police station, the suspect can get advice from a **lawyer**.

If a case goes to court for a **trial**, the suspect may be released on **bail** until the day of the trial. This means the suspect must turn up in court on the right date or face another charge. Suspects may have to ask someone they know to **guarantee** they will be at court. For most serious crimes, a jury will decide in court if the suspect is **guilty**. Then a judge must choose the punishment. It could mean prison.

## A warrant

Police do not always arrest suspects at the scene of a crime. The police may go to a suspect's home to arrest them. For this they need a **warrant**. This is an **official** written order allowing them to search a house or arrest someone.

Being arrested is the first step of the **legal** process.

A warrant allows police to go into a suspect's home without his or her permission.

jury group of people that hear the facts of a case to decide if a person is guilty
suspect someone thought to have committed a crime

# Going to court

A court case lets everyone involved have a say. The **defendant** should always get a fair **trial**. In serious cases a **jury** must look at all the evidence to get to the truth, guided by a judge. If the **verdict** is "guilty" the judge decides the punishment. It could be:

- a **fine**
- **probation** – where the **convicted** person is allowed home, but must report regularly to the authorities and prove good behaviour
- community service – where the convicted person must do a certain number of hours of work in the local community without pay
- a suspended sentence – where the convicted person does not go to prison if he or she keeps out of trouble for a set period of time
- a prison sentence.

## Longest criminal trial

The longest trial ever lasted for over a year. It took place in Hong Kong for 398 days, from 1992 to 1994. There were 14 **defendants charged** with murdering 24 people. All the defendants were finally found not guilty of murder.

Judges decide how criminals should be punished.

**fine** money owed as punishment for breaking the law
**probation** punishment instead of prison

## For all to see

Trials are public. People can go to watch, and news reporters in big cases describe what happens each day. Some courts in the United States allow trials to be broadcast on television.

The most watched court case ever was in 1995. Around 5.5 million people in the United States watched the live trial of O J Simpson. It lasted 9 months. O J Simpson was a famous American-football player and actor. He was charged with the murder of his ex-wife and a waiter. The jury reached a verdict of "not guilty" in October 1995. The charges were dropped and he was allowed to leave the courtroom a free man.

The O J Simpson trial was watched by millions of people from their own living rooms.

Mordecai Vanunu leaving prison after 12 years.

**verdict** decision reached by a jury – guilty or not guilty

15

## Innocent!

Every year people are released from prison because they have been found to be **innocent** after all. Robert McLaughlin was awarded a record US$2 million in 1989 for being jailed for a murder in New York City that he did not commit. He served 6 years in prison before the mistake was found.

# Getting locked up

Most people hate the thought of being locked up in prison. Prisons today are far more comfortable than they used to be, but they are definitely not the best places to spend your time. Even so, millions of people are behind bars all around the world. In the United States alone, there are over 2 million people in prison.

- More than 6 million people in the United States are on **parole** or **probation**.
- Every day in the USA, 200 new prison cells are built.
- The cost of keeping someone in prison for life in the United States is about US$1.5 million.

Prison life is shown in the film *The Shawshank Redemption*.

**Word Bank**     innocent  not guilty

# Tough life

All prisons are different. But all prisoners have something in common – time. They spend long hours locked up in their cells. No wonder some dream of breaking out.

A day could be like this:

**6.30 a.m.:** Getting up: breakfast.

**8.30 a.m.:** Activities: shower, exercise yard, visiting room, medical room, work, school or training.

**11.30 a.m.:** Back to cells.

**1.00 p.m.:** Lunch.

**1.30 p.m.:** Activities: shower, exercise yard, visiting room, work, school, or training.

**5.30 p.m.:** Back to cells.

**6.30 p.m.:** Evening meal then back to cells.

**10.00 p.m.:** Lights out.

This is a good day. Some days prisoners are stuck in their cells for up to 23 hours.

### Did you know?
- There are around 154 prisons in the UK.
- Each prisoner costs around £23,000 per year.
- There are about 71,000 prisoners in the UK.

San Quentin State Prison in California, USA has almost 6000 prisoners.

# Trying to get out

## Doing time

Prison cells were once cold, damp, and full of rats. In most countries today they are heated, and have a sink and a toilet. Most prisoners now have at least three showers a week and three meals a day. But that does not stop some of them trying to get out.

Ever since people were first locked up in prison, some have tried to get out. They may have dug a tunnel, made a hole through a wall, cut through bars, hidden in laundry, dressed as a guard, or used weapons. Many prisoners have failed to break out.

Mollie Brown was the first woman to try to escape from Joliet Prison, Chicago, USA. It was 1874 when Mollie was sent there for theft. A visitor smuggled in a **hacksaw** blade. Then Mollie made sure she misbehaved so she was sent up to a punishment cell for the night. This was all part of her plan.

Prison cells looked very different in the 13th century.

**Word Bank**    CCTV  close-circuit television. CCTV cameras are in most shops and high streets.

## Failure

The punishment cell was at the top of a tower. It had an iron bed, a mattress, and sheets. Mollie cut through the window bars with her blade. Then she made a rope out of ripped sheets. She thought the window opened over a roof. But there was a steep drop between two buildings. She could not see down in the darkness. As she climbed down to the end of her rope, Mollie found she was dangling high above the ground. Then the rope broke. Mollie fell and broke both legs and an arm. She also suffered **internal injuries**. She was soon behind bars again – in a far worse state than before.

### Top security

Prisons used to rely on bars, wire, and searchlights to stop **breakouts**. Today prisons use technology to stop prisoners escaping. Laser beams that sense movement, alarms, **CCTV** cameras, electrical locks, and **remote-controlled**, thick steel doors all keep prisoners safely locked away.

Mollie Brown is not the only prisoner to have tried to escape through a window.

Modern technology helps prison officers keep an eye on things.

internal injuries  pain or injury inside the body
remote-control  control, or work, from a distance

## Stuck in Alcatraz

Alcatraz Prison in San Francisco Bay is a famous old prison. It was built on a tiny island and was full of the worst criminals. The only way to escape was to swim across icy water full of dangerous currents. In almost 30 years as a prison, Alcatraz saw 14 escape attempts. In these escapes, 34 different **inmates** risked their lives to get off "the rock". Almost all of them were either killed or caught.

In 1937 two prisoners of Alcatraz, Theodore Cole and Ralph Roe, cut through iron bars and climbed out through a window. They made their way down to the water and disappeared into the bay. Fast currents and a bad storm swept them away. The two men were never seen again.

### Views from "the rock"

Alcatraz Island overlooks the Golden Gate Bridge of San Francisco, USA. Today, over a million tourists visit the closed-down prison each year. At one time prisoners tried anything to get away from it. From 1934 to 1963 it was one of the toughest prisons in the world.

Alcatraz Prison was nicknamed "the rock".

**Word Bank**   inmate member of a group living in a single building, such as a prison

## Good try

John Giles saw his chance to escape from Alcatraz in 1945. One of his jobs was to unload the army's laundry when it was sent to the island to be cleaned. He stole an army uniform to dress as a soldier and he walked out of the prison. He calmly walked on to an army boat to what he thought was freedom. He hoped to get off in San Francisco and vanish into the crowd. Instead, the boat went to Angel Island where prison officers were waiting after they noticed Giles was missing. They took him back to Alcatraz. A good try – but not good enough!

> " Alcatraz was never any good for anybody. "
>
> Frank Wathernam, the last prisoner to leave Alcatraz (21 March 1963)

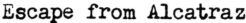

## Escape from Alcatraz

The most famous escape attempt from Alcatraz was in 1962. Three men broke out of the prison. They were Frank Morris, John Anglin, and his brother Clarence Anglin. They vanished from their cells, never to be seen again.

The men used home-made drills on the air vent in their cell wall to make the vent bigger. By hiding the hole with bricks, they kept the guards from knowing what was going on. When the hole was big enough for them to squeeze through, they were ready to escape. One night they put dummy heads on their pillows to make the guards think they were fast asleep.

### The film

The 1979 film *Escape from Alcatraz* tells the true story of how three men escaped from the **maximum-**security prison. Clint Eastwood plays Frank Morris, who got away from the island – never to be seen again.

Clint Eastwood as Frank Morris.

The film *Escape from Alcatraz* shows how hard prison life can be.

**Word Bank**     **identify** find out or show who someone is

## Up and away

The three men got out through the air vent and climbed up on to the roof of the cell block. They climbed down a drainpipe to the water's edge. They used prison raincoats to make life jackets and a small raft to help them stay afloat.

Prison guards found the drills, the hole in the wall and two home-made life jackets in the water. But there was no sign of the men. Weeks later a man's body was found along the coast dressed like the prisoners. The body was in such a bad state that it could not be **identified**. It was probably one of the escaped prisoners.

### Break-up

The salt water around Alcatraz began to eat away at the prison walls. It would have taken US$5 million dollars to repair Alcatraz. In the 1960s, it cost:

- US$9.27 a day to keep an **inmate** in a mainland prison
- US$23.50 a day for each inmate on Alcatraz.

So in 1963, Alcatraz had to close.

Today, Alcatraz is a museum visited by millions of people each year.

**maximum** highest possible

## Sing Sing Prison

In 1929, prisoners dug a 15-metre (49-foot) long tunnel under the wall of Sing Sing Prison in New York, USA. They dumped all the dirt by scattering it around the yard. Guards had no idea what was going on until they found the tunnel during a search. The **guilty** prisoners were each sent to other prisons.

The next **breakout** plot was in 1941. Three men broke out of the hospital on the third floor of the prison, using guns that had been smuggled in. They killed a prison guard and ran down to the basement. From there they climbed through a vent, out into the street where friends had a car waiting.

### Still going strong

New York's famous Sing Sing Prison was built in 1825. Over 180 years later, it still locks away some of the United States's most dangerous criminals. Very few have ever escaped.

Sing Sing is a famous US prison.

**Word Bank**     **executed** put to death

## Caught

Just as the men were getting into the car, two police officers arrived. There was a shoot-out. One prisoner was shot dead and one policeman was killed. By now the prison breakout was big news so the two prisoners had to get away quickly. They stole a boat to cross the Hudson River and then ran into woods to hide. Police used a pack of dogs to hunt them down.

The two men, Riordan and McGale, were caught and sent to trial for killing the policeman. They were found guilty of murder and **executed** at Sing Sing, the very place they had been so desperate to leave.

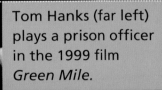

Tom Hanks (far left) plays a prison officer in the 1999 film *Green Mile*.

# The Great Train Robbery

In the 1960s, the UK's Great Train Robbery was big news. So were the events that followed!

## Crime of the century

In 1963 a large gang of robbers held up a train near London. They stole £2.6 million. The Great Train Robbery was the UK's robbery of the century. Within a year, all seventeen gang members had been tracked down and were behind bars. At least, for a while…

## Great Train Robber escapes from prison (1964)

A gang of three men broke into Winson Green Prison last night and freed Charlie Wilson, one of the Great Train Robbers. They broke into the grounds of a hospital next to the prison. They climbed the 6-metre (20-foot) high prison wall and tied up one of the guards. It is still not known how they got hold of the keys to Wilson's cell. The prison is high security and only one member of staff holds the cell keys at night.

Charlie Wilson was caught in Canada 4 years later.

Ronnie Biggs was one of the train robbers to escape from prison.

**Word Bank**     abandoned left behind

## Ronnie Biggs escapes from prison (1965)

Ronald Biggs, 35, a member of the Great Train Robbery gang, has escaped from Wandsworth Prison, London. He climbed a ladder over a 10-metre (33-foot) high wall with three other prisoners. Friends from outside threw the ladder over the wall when the prisoners were in the exercise yard. They jumped down to waiting cars and were driven away.

Police later found a car used in the escape. It was **abandoned** outside a nearby railway station. There was a loaded shotgun and a set of prison clothes inside.

Ronnie Biggs escaped to Brazil and stayed there for 36 years.

### Back behind bars

Ronnie Biggs returned to the UK in 2001, aged 71, and gave himself up. He was ill after a series of **strokes** and came back for medical treatment. He was taken to prison to serve the remaining 28 years of his sentence.

The Great Train Robbery was made into a film.

As an old man, Ronnie Biggs returned to the UK.

**stroke** sudden illness caused when blood cannot reach the brain

## The Texas Seven

In 2000, seven **inmates** at the Connally prison near Kenedy, Texas, USA, made a shocking **breakout**. Armed with a small screwdriver and a knife blade, they attacked guards and took their weapons. The gang took overalls to hide their prison uniforms. Then they stole a truck and guns. They left a note saying: "You haven't heard the last of us yet."

The Texas Seven drove out of the prison's back gate and down the road to freedom. It was the start of one of the largest **manhunts** in US history.

## Manhunt

A week later, on Christmas Eve, the escaped gang held up a gun shop and stole more guns. Police Officer Hawkins rushed to the scene, but they shot him dead. A reward was offered for the men. It reached US$500,000. A month later, the story appeared on the television show *America's Most Wanted*.

### 21st-century breakout

How could seven prisoners escape all at once? The men were violent and attacked the prison guards. They took **hostages** and stole their clothes. They got away before the alarm was raised. Although they enjoyed Christmas away from prison, it was far from a happy ending for the criminals.

The seven prisoners who escaped in Texas in 2000.

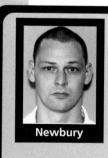
Newbury

Rivas

Rodriguez

Garcia

Halprin

Murphy

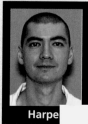
Harpe

**Word Bank**   **hostage** person taken and held for a reason, such as to stop police from shooting

The owner of a **trailer park** was watching and knew the men were in his park. He told the police and four of the gang were arrested. Another killed himself. The last two men were caught soon afterwards. Their freedom did not last long.

## Penalty

The ringleader of the Texas Seven was George Rivas (above). He went on **trial** for the breakout and the murder of a police officer. It took a week for the jury to think about the evidence and **convict** him. Rivas said that he deserved to die for the death of Police Officer Hawkins. The jury agreed and sentenced him to death.

Despite the high security at Connally prison, the Texas Seven escaped.

**manhunt** organized search for someone, usually a criminal
**trailer park** caravan site

# In the news

Stories of **breakouts** and **blunders** continue to fill the news. True crime keeps attracting true idiots!

Two prisoners who escaped from Bowie County Jail, Texas, USA, on 28 January 2004 will pay a heavy price for a few hours of freedom. They now face spending far longer in prison after their weekend escape.

The two men attacked a guard and escaped from a van taking them to another jail. During their run, they **kidnapped** three people, stole three vehicles and robbed a shop. They then got lost and ended up miles from anywhere before they were captured and put back in prison.

## We're off

In 2004, two prisoners escaped from a police station in Winifreda, Argentina, by unscrewing their cell door and running off. Before they escaped, they left a note for the police officers:

> We love our freedom and can't live locked in. We're sorry for any problem we might have caused you.

Even criminals can have good manners!

Some prisoners at Adelaide prison thought they could come and go through the wire as they pleased!

**Word Bank**

kidnap  carry off a person by force, or against his or her wi

## Just popping out

Can you believe anyone would want to break out of prison and then break back in again? That is just what some **inmates** did at Adelaide prison, Australia, in 2004. They climbed over the prison fence to meet friends and to buy drugs. But to avoid getting into trouble, they climbed back into prison before they were found to be missing! This happened a few times before guards found out what was going on.

### Mass breakout

In October 2004, seven inmates shot their way out of a prison near Mexico City. They escaped in waiting cars. Hundreds of police rushed to the prison to stop any more of the 3000 prisoners held there from escaping. Six inmates escaped from the same prison six months earlier, but only three were caught.

During a **manhunt** police often use helicopters to help them search.

**inmates** member of a group living in a single building, such as a prison

## Escape attempt falls through

In September 2003, a prisoner was about to appear in court in Decatur, Georgia, USA, when he thought he would try to escape. Ben Rogozensky went to the toilets just before his **trial** and climbed out through the ceiling tiles. Just as he was crawling through the roof, he fell right through the ceiling. He landed in a heap in the judge's office. Staff grabbed him before he could get any further. Instead of getting away, he had to appear in court yet again – to face an escape charge. Unlike him, the **charge** was not dropped!

Sniffer dogs track down escaped criminals.

**sniffer dog** police dog trained to follow the smell of drugs, criminals, or explosives

## Caught red-handed

In October 2004, a **sniffer dog** followed a trail of blood from the scene of a crime to a hospital. A 21-year-old man had broken into a computer shop in Ludwigslust, Germany. He cut his hand after smashing a window to get in. He stole several computers.

The police set sniffer dog Rex to work and he followed a trail to a nearby flat. The trail then led to a local hospital where the thief had gone for treatment. The police said: "He was stunned when we turned up with the sniffer dog. He admitted the theft straight away."

### The longest prison escape

Leonard Fristoe killed two police officers in 1920 and went to prison for his crime. He escaped from Nevada State prison, USA, 3 years later. He stayed free for 46 years until his own son turned him in. He went back to prison in 1969!

Leonard Fristoe being led back to prison 46 years after he was arrested.

## Not too clever

Some criminals are not too clever. The biggest **blunder** they make is to get up in the morning!

In August 1998, the police in Brunswick, Georgia, USA were looking for a handbag-snatcher. They picked up a man who looked **suspicious**. They drove him to the scene of the crime to see if the victim would recognize him. He got out of the car to face the woman. The **suspect** did as he was told, looked at the victim very carefully and blurted out: "Yeah, that's the woman I robbed."

### Dumb thief

Police in Australia released a **suspect** from the police station in 1999. He ran round the corner and jumped into a car. The keys were inside so off he went. Stupidly, the man had stolen a police squad car. Police began a high-speed chase. He was soon arrested again!

Victims sometimes **identify** criminals from a line up.

Australian police on the trail.

# Caught on camera

In 2002 a man smashed a bank door in Marked Tree, Arkansas, USA. He was angry it was shut, because it meant he could not rob it. So he grabbed handfuls of lollipops from a display in the window. Police followed a trail of lollipop wrappers down the street to a **trailer park** where the man was staying. They knew he was the criminal because he had looked right into the bank's security cameras when he set off the alarm. The police recognized him as he had also stolen rings from a jewellery shop. But they were just plastic fakes. The police said, "This man is not the brightest chip on the block."

## Nice neighbours!

After an armed robbery at a petrol station in Perth, Australia, police did not have to go far to find the suspect. "It's the man next door," the petrol station attendant said. "He tried to cover his head with his jacket but I knew it was him." Police went next door and arrested a 19-year-old counting the AUS $1200 he had just taken from the petrol station!

suspicious acting in a guilty way

## Unlucky

For prisoners to escape, they need a lot of luck. They do not always get it!

In 1998, Martin Gurule escaped from Ellis Prison, Texas, USA. With six other **inmates**, he put dummies in their beds to fool prison guards. They dyed their white prison clothes with felt-tip pens and crawled through the roof at night. Gurule was the only one to get out. Guards caught the others before they could climb the fence. Gurule dodged gunfire and got over the **razor wire** by wrapping himself in cardboard. But his luck ran out. He tried to swim across the nearby Trinity River and drowned.

### Caught on camera

A pair of bank robbers tried to make their getaway in Calgary, Canada, in 1999. They ran into some bad luck. They became instant film stars when they crashed onto a street that was being used as a film set!

Smile, you've just been caught on camera!

## Stolen ring found

It took a long time and some strong medicine for police to get back a stolen diamond ring worth US$10,000. Kevin Lynch of Boston, USA, stole the ring from a jeweller's shop in 2004. The only trouble was, he swallowed it so he would not get caught!

An X-ray showed the ring was stuck in his stomach. So how could the police get it back? Doctors gave Lynch medicine to move things along. The police then had to wait for him to go to the toilet and then search the results. It was not the best of jobs. At last they found the ring in one piece. All part of police work!

razor wire  wire covered in sharp spikes

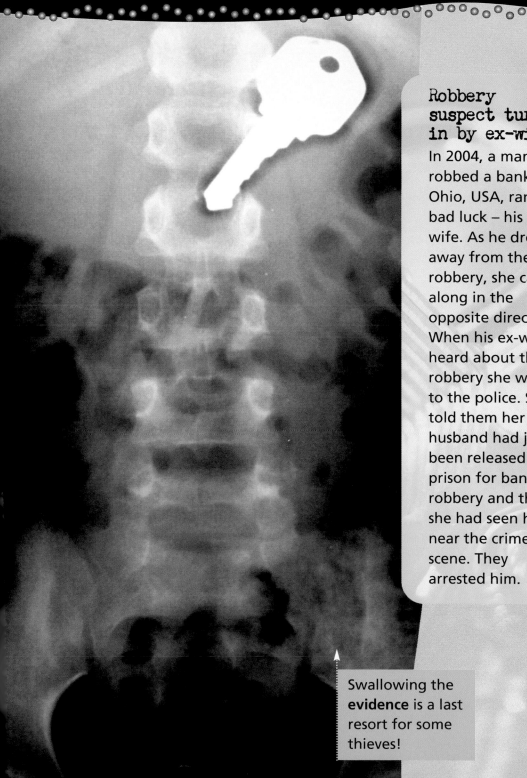

## Robbery suspect turned in by ex-wife

In 2004, a man who robbed a bank in Ohio, USA, ran into bad luck – his ex-wife. As he drove away from the robbery, she came along in the opposite direction. When his ex-wife heard about the robbery she went to the police. She told them her ex-husband had just been released from prison for bank robbery and that she had seen him near the crime scene. They arrested him.

Swallowing the **evidence** is a last resort for some thieves!

evidence  statements or objects used in a trial to help prove guilt or innocence

## Stuck in church

Police were called to a church in High Point, North Carolina, USA in 2002 when a thief got stuck in a window. Ronald Stutts was firmly wedged. It took four policemen to get him out. He had got in through a large window and was trying to get out through a much smaller one. He was arrested for breaking and entering.

## Trapped!

In Houston, Texas, USA, it was soon after Christmas 2003 when a thief tried Santa's way of breaking in. Michael Arlington tried to rob a restaurant at night by climbing down the chimney. He got stuck! Arlington used his mobile phone to call a friend for help. The friend came and broke a window, but ran away when the alarm went off.

Police arrived to find Arlington's legs dangling from the fireplace. Firefighters went up on the roof and lowered a rope, which Arlington was able to climb up. He was sentenced to 6 months in prison for **attempted burglary**.

Firefighters had to come to the rescue when a burglar got stuck in a chimney!

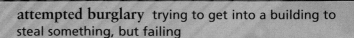
attempted burglary  trying to get into a building to steal something, but failing

# Clumsy thief falls in bin

What would it be like to fall into a bottle bank or one of the large bins that many towns use to recycle waste? Some recycle bins are for old clothes. But it is not wise to try and steal a jacket from one. Someone did in 2004.

In Bochum, Germany, a 43-year-old thief tried to reach into a clothes bin and he fell right in. People heard cries from inside. Police and firefighters had to rescue him. They arrived to see just the man's arms sticking out of the top of the bin. The flap on the opening only opened one way so he could not get out again.

> We know you're in there!

## Thief locks himself in car

A 51-year-old thief was arrested after he got locked inside the car he was trying to steal in Florida in 2002. The car **automatically** locked the doors when the car alarm went off. When police arrived, they found the thief hiding down by the back seat.

## Security blunders

It is not always the criminal that gets things wrong. The police and security services have made silly mistakes, too.

In Scotland, in 2004, a security company freed five prisoners by mistake. The company had the job of taking prisoners to court from their cells. Somehow they lost them! The company used secure vans that no one could escape from. The problem was that staff just let them go. Even a **convicted** killer was allowed to walk free.

### "Sorry, wrong house."

In May 2003, residents of a block of flats in the Bronx area of New York City, USA, got a loud wake-up call from a police drug **squad**. Officers burst into their homes, waved guns and handcuffs at them. Then they said "Sorry, wrong house." Someone had a lot of explaining to do!

Prisoners are usually kept secure in special vans.

**Word Bank** **residents** people who live in a certain place. Your family are the residents of your home.

# Police kick in wrong door!

Police kicked down a door in Gateshead, UK, in an early morning raid in 2004 – only to find they were 8 kilometres (5 miles) from the correct address. Police broke through the door at 3.15 a.m. They made a fast exit when they were told the crime was at the same address – but in another town! **Innocent** people asleep in their beds were shocked to find the police bursting into their house.

Police admitted the **blunder**, but blamed reports of wrong information from the public for the mix-up. It always pays to check the facts.

## Silly mistake

In 2004, some German prison guards made a bit of a mistake. When they released a bank robber from prison, they handed him back his gun. He then used it in another robbery. The 42-year-old man was caught trying to hold up a bank in Krefeld, Germany. A prison **spokesperson** said: "We don't know how this could have happened."

Smashing down doors at the wrong house is a terrible police blunder!

spokesperson someone who speaks on behalf of an organization

## Look before you leap

Isaac Mofokeng, a robber armed with a gun, ran away from the police in South Africa in 1997. He foolishly tried to hide in a zoo. He jumped over a wall and ended up inside the gorilla pen. Max, the gorilla, was not happy. He grabbed the robber, ripped his jeans and bit him on the buttocks. Then he jumped on him and hit him. Mofokeng shot Max in the jaw and shoulder. Luckily the police arrived before Mofokeng could do any more harm. He was arrested and sent to prison for 40 years.

Max the gorilla became an instant hero. Everyone praised his bravery. After surgery, Max made a full recovery and lived until 2004.

## Burglar arrested after getaway scooter stolen

In 2004 a burglar parked his getaway scooter outside a jeweller's shop in Nanterre, France. He broke in, armed with a gun. When he ran out, his scooter had been stolen. He was furious that no one could be trusted anymore! Police arrived and took him to the police station. An officer said: "At least he is in the right place to report the stolen scooter!"

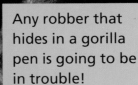

Any robber that hides in a gorilla pen is going to be in trouble!

**Word Bank**   **cubicle** small space, usually big enough for one person
**fiction** not true, a made-up story

# Stranger than fiction

Many crime stories seem too crazy to be true. Who would want to steal a public toilet, and why? For some reason, thieves did just that in the city of Gomel, Belarus in 2004. A gang loaded the **portable** toilet on to their trailer and took it away. But there was a problem. A man was sitting on the toilet at the time!

The man was trapped until the rope tied around the **cubicle** worked loose. He opened the door to find he was going at full speed through the city. He jumped out and broke his collarbone.

## Human error

The world of crime is full of strange stories. True crime is often stranger then fiction. This is because criminals do the craziest of things. Sometimes the police do, too. After all, we all make mistakes!

Police and criminals make **blunders** – they are only human after all!

# Find out more

If you want to find out more about the criminal underworld, why not have a look at these books:

*Behind the Scenes: Solving a Crime*,
Peter Mellet (Heinemann Library, 1999)
*Forensic Files: Investigating Murders*,
Paul Dowswell (Heinemann Library, 2004)
*Forensic Files: Investigating Thefts and Heists*,
Alex Woolf (Heinemann Library, 2004)
*Just the Facts: Cyber Crime*,
Neil McIntosh (Heinemann Library, 2002)

## Man on the run asks police the way

A Romanian who tried to cross a border in 2004 was arrested after asking an off-duty policeman for directions. He even boasted that he was on the run from police. The policeman said: "He asked me how far it was to the border and then told me he was going to make an **illegal** crossing. I pretended I was going to take him there, but took him to my police colleagues instead."

## Did you know?

- In the UK, crime costs at least £60 billion per year, compared to the £1.9 billion cost of running the prison service.

- In the United States, Colorado's "Supermax" prison has the latest equipment to stop **breakouts**. It has special detectors to sense any movement. There are laser beams, 1400 **remote-controlled** steel doors, pressure pads, and dogs that are trained to attack. Prisoners spend 23 hours a day locked in their cells and are only allowed outside in leg-irons and handcuffs.

- During the American Civil War, 109 prisoners escaped through a tunnel from Libby Prison on 9 February 1864. It was called "The Great Escape".

**Breaking out of prison is nothing new...**

25 July 1724: Jack Sheppard, a burglar, who escaped from New-Prison in London, UK, is sent to Newgate Prison. He is charged with several thefts.

17 October 1724: Jack Sheppard makes yet another escape from prison.

2 November 1724: Jack Sheppard is captured.

16 November 1724: Jack Sheppard is hanged.

# Glossary

**abandoned** left behind

**attempted burglary** trying to get into a building to steal something, but failing

**automatically** working by itself

**bail** release of a person waiting to be on trial for a crime

**blunder** silly mistake, when things go wrong

**breakout** escape

**bribe** something given to a person, usually money, to make them do something dishonest

**bungle** make a mistake

**career** job or skill that can last a person's working life

**CCTV** close-circuit television. CCTV cameras are in most shops and high streets.

**charge** formal blame for a crime

**convicted** found guilty of committing a crime

**cubicle** small space, usually big enough for one person

**defendant** person on trial for a crime

**disguise** change the way you look to hide from, or fool, other people

**disturbance** something that upsets people or causes harm

**evidence** statements or objects used in a trial to help prove guilt or innocence

**executed** put to death

**fiction** not true, a made-up story

**fine** money owed as punishment for breaking the law

**getaway** escape

**guarantee** a promise to make sure something happens

**guilty** done something wrong

**hacksaw** saw with a thin blade, for cutting metal

**hostage** person taken and held for a reason, such as to stop police shooting

**identify** find out or show who someone is

**illegal** against the law

**inmate** member of a group living in a single building, such as a prison

**innocent** not guilty

**internal injuries** pain or injury inside the body

**jury** group of people that hear the facts of a case to decide if a person is guilty

**kidnap** carry off a person by force, or against his or her will

**lawyer** person who is paid to give help and advice on legal matters

**legal** allowed by law

**manhunt** organized search for someone, usually a criminal

**maximum** highest possible

**offence** crime, something that breaks the law

**official** ordered by an authority

**parole** early release of a well-behaved prisoner

**portable** able to be carried or moved

**probation** punishment instead of prison

**razorwire** (also called "barbed wire") wire covered in sharp spikes

**remote-control** control, or work, from a distance

**residents** people who live in a certain place. Your family are the residents of your home.

**spokesperson** someone who speaks on behalf of an organization

**squad** small group of officers

**sniffer dog** police dog trained to follow the smell of drugs, criminals, or explosives

**stroke** sudden illness caused when blood cannot reach the brain

**suspect** someone thought to have committed a crime

**suspicious** acting in a guilty way

**trailer park** caravan site

**trial** time in court when the facts of a case are given. The jury decide at the trial if the suspect is guilty.

**verdict** decision reached by a jury – guilty or not guilty

**warrant** official written order allowing police to make a search or an arrest

# Index

# Titles in the *True Crime* series include:

Hardback: 1844 438120

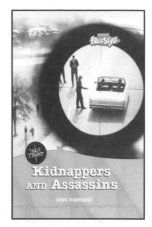

Hardback: 1844 438112

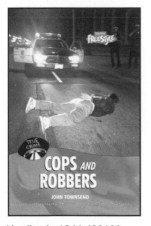

Hardback: 1844 438139

Hardback: 1844 438104

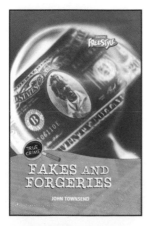

Hardback: 1844 438090

Find out about other Freestyle titles on our website www.raintreepublishers.co.uk